Cupcakes
from the Primrose Bakery

Cupcakes
from the Primrose Bakery

Martha Swift
&
Lisa Thomas

Photography by Yuki Sugiura

Kyle Books

For Daisy and Millie, Thomas and Ned

Kyle Books
An imprint of Kyle Cathie Limited
www.kylebooks.com
Distributed by National Books Network
(800) 462-6420

First published in Great Britain in 2009 by
Kyle Cathie Limited

ISBN 978-1-906868-08-6

Photographer Yuki Sugiura *
Illustrations Michael Heath
Designer Nicky Collings
Props Stylist Cynthia Inions
Food Stylist Linda Tubby
Project Editor Sophie Allen
Copy Editor Stephanie Evans
Proofreader Ruth Baldwin
Production Gemma John

* except for author photograph on page 8: Elizabeth Scheder-Bieschin

A Cataloging in Publication record for this title is available from the Library of Congress.

Color reproduction by Colourscan
Printed in China by C&C Offset Printing Co., Ltd.

Contents

Introduction

In October 2004 we started baking cupcakes for children's parties in Primrose Hill, North London. We were two mothers, each with two young children. We had discovered that the kind of cupcakes we had in mind – tasting as delicious as they looked and looking as good as they tasted – were not to be found. It also quickly became clear to us that the cupcakes we made were being eaten as much by the adults as by the children. We knew that cupcakes were very popular in Australia and America: why not in the UK? Their simplicity and versatility make them perfect for almost every occasion or just everyday. You can make as many or as few as you need and decorate them extravagantly or totally simply. Most people, of every age, sex, and background seem to enjoy eating them!

Our idea was very simple. We wanted to produce cupcakes from natural ingredients, using no preservatives and no artificial colors, ingredients, or flavors. And, equally important, we wanted them to look amazing and totally distinctive. To do this, we knew we had to find the decorations outside the UK. We went to the US, to Italy, to Australia, and to the Philippines in search of original and appealing sugar cake decorations – flowers, sprinkles, animals, butterflies. This has since grown to take in decorations for every possible occasion and public holiday – from Valentine's Day to Halloween, from Mother's Day to Christmas Day.

Our first cupcakes were baked at home, in a domestic oven in Lisa's kitchen (which was always full of children) in between the school run and the ironing. Soon after selling our cupcakes to a local delicatessen, Melrose and Morgan in Primrose Hill, on a daily basis, we were approached by Selfridges Food Hall. We became their first supplier of cupcakes and their first supplier from a domestic kitchen. Since then we have expanded to sell to Fortnum and Mason and other major food stores. Because our cupcakes are all made with natural ingredients we were also able to start supplying organic markets.

Very early on we began to get orders for private functions. At first, these mainly took the shape of children's parties, christenings, and birthdays. But quickly we were asked to provide cupcakes for every other kind of event, both private and public. We have done book launches with themes, such as all-orange mini cupcakes for the Orange Prize for Fiction. We have supplied cupcakes for designers for Fashion Week. We made cupcakes for Elton John's 60th birthday party and for the Brits music

introduction

awards. We are lucky enough to work on a regular basis with outstanding British fashion brands such as Anya Hindmarch, LK Bennett, Miller Harris, Topshop, and Paul Smith. Each time the cupcakes are tailored to the occasion and the demands of our customers. And we have developed an alternative to the traditional wedding cake, in the form of pyramids of cupcakes, frosted and decorated with flowers, both sugar and fresh. We now cater to occasions all over southern England.

In the autumn of 2006 we realized that we had outgrown Lisa's kitchen. We opened our first bakery and café in Primrose Hill, baking everything on site. We wanted to create an environment to go with the cupcakes – customers can come for freshly baked croissants, cupcakes, and cookies while having excellent coffee and tea. The smells rising from the kitchen below bring people in from the whole neighborhood. We have kept to our original idea: everything is baked and frosted by hand and every cupcake is individual. In November 2008 we opened our second shop in Tavistock Street in Covent Garden, run along the same principles as our first shop, with all the cupcakes and other pastries baked in the basement and a small café on the ground floor so that customers may eat in or take away.

Nearly five years on, we are still determined to hold on to our idea of a home-baking, less industrial type of bakery. Our recipes are straightforward and can be made in ordinary kitchens with no special equipment or skills. In this book we show how easy it is to produce – in a world increasingly given over to production lines and fancy packaging – a cupcake that is delicious, pretty, and without artificial ingredients. We always recommend using seasonal and well-sourced ingredients as it makes such a difference to the finished product.

It is not simply about cupcakes. It is about producing food that is different – that looks different and tastes different. It is about food that smells delicious and that you want to eat. Cupcakes suit any and every occasion and every imaginable person, from a five-year-old to a bride, from proud new parents to celebrating octogenarians. We want to demonstrate how, if you believe in these ideas, if you follow these simple recipes, it can be both pleasurable and rewarding.

Basic Cupcakes

Much of the appeal of cupcakes lies in the relative ease with which they can be prepared, and their versatility. Four basic cupcake cake batters – vanilla, chocolate, lemon, and carrot – can be made in any quantity, frosted with a variety of buttercreams, and dressed up or down, as the occasion demands. These basics are a great place to start if you are new to baking or to which you can return time and time again, however experienced a baker you are.

To guarantee a perfect cupcake, these are the golden rules we always follow: First, always use good-quality ingredients and bring everything to room temperature before you start to mix them. Try also to be very precise with measuring. Always sift the flour and leavenings to avoid lumps. We advise you to use an electric hand mixer if possible, as one makes it so much quicker and easier to beat the ingredients together and to get a good consistency, but obviously you can beat the mixtures by hand, if you wish. And, to ensure all those carefully measured ingredients end up as cake, use a rubber spatula to scrape down the sides of the bowl to ensure the batter mixture is well combined. Next, it's just as important to be accurate with the oven temperatures and cooking times and – as with pretty much all baking – don't be tempted to open the oven door while the cupcakes are baking as even a small amount of cold air tends to make the batter fall. Lastly, when you turn out your cupcakes, do allow them to cool completely before frosting and, if possible, frost and eat them on the same day, when the cake is at its freshest. Alternatively the cupcakes can be stored in airtight containers before frosting. They will keep for up to three days at room temperature. Do not refrigerate.

Vanilla Cupcakes

This is our classic cupcake; it takes a lead role in our kitchens with its huge versatility as it can be dressed in a variety of frostings and adorned with decorations that will take it from one occasion to another.

Preheat the oven to 350°F and line a 12-cup muffin pan or three 12-cup mini muffin pans with cupcake liners.

In a large mixing bowl cream the butter and sugar until the mixture is pale and smooth, which should take 3–5 minutes using an electric hand mixer. Add the eggs, one at a time, mixing for a few minutes after each addition.

Sift the two flours together into a separate bowl. Mix the milk and vanilla together.

Add one-third of the flours to the creamed mixture and beat well. Pour in one-third of the milk and beat again. Repeat these steps until all the flour and milk have been added.

Carefully spoon the mixture into the cups, filling them about two-thirds full. Bake in the oven for 20-25 minutes (regular size) or 15 minutes (mini size) until slightly raised and golden brown. To check they are cooked, insert a wooden skewer in the center of one of the cupcakes – it should come out clean.

Remove from the oven and leave the cupcakes in the pan for about 10 minutes before carefully placing on a wire rack to cool. Once they are completely cool, frost the cupcakes with vanilla, chocolate, or lime and coconut buttercream frosting.

Makes 12 regular or
36 mini cupcakes

**8 tablespoons unsalted butter,
   at room temperature**
**1 cup plus 2 tablespoons sugar,
   preferably golden bakers'**
2 large eggs, free-range or organic
1 cup self-rising flour
**¾ cup plus 1 tablespoon
   all-purpose flour**
**½ cup 2% reduced-fat milk,
   at room temperature**
1 teaspoon pure vanilla extract

Chocolate Cupcakes

Always a favorite, these moist chocolate cupcakes are great, made regular size or as minis. They can be used with a number of our buttercreams, making them all the more delicious!

Makes 16 regular or 48 mini cupcakes

4oz bittersweet chocolate (70% cocoa solids)
6 tablespoons unsalted butter, at room temperature
¾ cup packed light brown sugar
2 large eggs, free-range or organic, separated
1¼ cups all-purpose flour
¾ teaspoon baking powder
¾ teaspoon baking soda
Pinch of salt
1 cup 2% reduced-fat milk, at room temperature
1 teaspoon pure vanilla extract

Preheat the oven to 375°F and line 16 cups in two 12-cup muffin pans or four 12-cup mini muffin pans with cupcake liners.

Break the chocolate into pieces and melt. The easiest way is to put it in a microwave-safe bowl in a microwave on medium heat for 30 seconds, stir, and then microwave again for a further 30 seconds – but be very careful not to burn the chocolate. Alternatively, put the pieces in a heatproof bowl over a saucepan of barely simmering water. Stir occasionally until it has completely melted and is quite smooth. Leave to cool slightly.

In a large bowl cream the butter and sugar until the mixture is pale and smooth, which should take 3–5 minutes using an electric hand mixer. In a separate bowl and with clean beaters, beat the egg yolks for several minutes. Slowly add the egg yolks to the creamed mixture and beat well. Next, add the melted chocolate to the mixture and beat well.

Sift the flour, baking powder, baking soda, and salt together into a separate bowl. Mix the milk and vanilla together. Add one-third of the flour to the chocolate mixture and beat well. Pour in one-third of the milk and beat again. Repeat these steps until all the flour and milk have been added. In a clean bowl with clean beaters, whip the egg whites until soft peaks start to form. Carefully fold the egg whites into the batter, using a metal spoon. Do not beat or you will take all the air out of the batter.

Carefully spoon the mixture into the cups, filling them about two-thirds full. Bake in the oven for 20–25 minutes (regular size) or 15 minutes (mini size). To check they are cooked, insert a wooden skewer in the center of one of the cupcakes – it should come out clean. Remove from the oven and leave the cupcakes in the pans for about 10 minutes before carefully placing on a wire rack to cool. Once they are completely cool, frost the cupcakes with chocolate, vanilla, or coffee buttercream.

These cupcakes can be stored at room temperature for 3 days in an airtight container before frosting. They are very moist, so they keep very well if stored correctly.

Lemon Cupcakes

These fresh lemon cupcakes are always very popular in our bakery and also at weddings and christenings. Make sure you use really plump juicy lemons for maximum zing!

Preheat the oven to 350°F and line a 12-cup muffin pan with cupcake liners.

In a large mixing bowl cream the butter and sugar until the mixture is pale and smooth, which should take 3–5 minutes using an electric hand mixer. Add the eggs, one at a time, mixing for a few minutes after each addition.

Sift the two flours together into a separate bowl. Mix the milk, lemon juice, and sour cream together. Add one-third of the flours to the creamed mixture and beat well. Pour in one-third of the milk and beat again. Repeat these steps until all the flour and milk have been added, incorporating the lemon zest with the last third of flour. Don't worry if the mixture starts to curdle: simply add another spoonful of all-purpose flour and beat well.

Carefully spoon the mixture into the cups, filling them about two-thirds full. Bake in the oven for about 25 minutes until slightly raised and golden brown. To check they are cooked, insert a wooden skewer in the center of one of the cupcakes – it should come out clean.

Remove from the oven and leave the cupcakes in the pan for about 10 minutes before carefully placing on a wire rack to cool. Once they are completely cool, frost the cupcakes with lemon buttercream and decorate with a candied lemon slice or a little finely grated lemon zest.

Makes 12 regular cupcakes

8 tablespoons unsalted butter,
    at room temperature
1 cup plus 2 tablespoons sugar,
    preferably golden bakers'
2 large eggs, free-range or organic
1 cup self-rising flour
¾ cup plus 1 tablespoon
    all-purpose flour
⅓ cup 2% reduced-fat milk,
    at room temperature
2 tablespoons freshly squeezed
    lemon juice
1 tablespoon sour cream
Grated zest of 1 lemon (you need
    1 teaspoon)

Carrot Cupcakes

With all those carrots and raisins, these moist little cakes feel like they must be good for you! They can be eaten warm as a great start to your morning or topped with our orange cream cheese frosting (see page 35). They are also perfect for a less sweet afternoon treat.

Preheat the oven to 350°F and line a 12-cup muffin pan with cupcake liners.

Peel and finely grate the carrots and drain off any liquid. Combine the grated carrots and raisins in a large bowl using a wooden spoon and set aside.

In a large mixing bowl beat the eggs and sugar together for several minutes and then add the oil, vanilla extract, and orange zest and beat well.

Sift the flour, baking soda, salt, and cinnamon together in a separate bowl. Gradually add these ingredients to the egg and sugar mixture, beating well after each addition. Pour this mixture into the bowl containing the carrots and raisins and incorporate using a wooden spoon or spatula until they are evenly blended.

Carefully spoon the mixture into the cups, filling them about two-thirds full. Bake in the oven for about 25 minutes – the cupcakes will be quite dark brown in color and feel "spongy" to the touch. Remove from the oven and leave the cupcakes in the pans for about 10 minutes before carefully placing on a wire rack to cool.

These cupcakes often look a bit smaller than some of the other recipes and are deliciously moist and dense. If you are frosting them with orange cream cheese frosting, it's nice to finish them off with a sprinkling of cinnamon.

Makes about
12 regular cupcakes

8oz (4 medium) carrots
1 cup seedless raisins
2 large eggs, free-range or organic
⅔ cup sugar, preferably
golden bakers'
½ cup corn oil
½ teaspoon pure vanilla extract
Grated zest of 1 orange (you
need 2 teaspoons)
¾ cup all-purpose flour
1 teaspoon baking soda
Pinch of salt
1 teaspoon ground cinnamon

Basic Frostings

The secret to perfect buttercream frosting is to beat the mixture for long enough (preferably with an electric hand mixer), which is always much longer than you might imagine! Aim to beat your frosting for several minutes until it is very smooth and creamy. Sifting the confectioners' sugar before using it also helps to ensure the ideal consistency.

The ingredients for these six basic buttercream frosting recipes are simple and few, but by choosing high-quality pure vanilla extract, bittersweet chocolate, and espresso powder, and selecting ripe and juicy citrus fruit, you will ensure a fantastic end result.

Buttercream frosting should always be stored in airtight containers at room temperature and – apart from the cream cheese frosting – never refrigerated. It keeps well for up to three days and so it can be used with one type of cupcake one day and another the next. Simply beat the frosting again with an electric hand mixer or a wooden spoon to get it to the right consistency before using.

How to frost a cupcake

Practice makes perfect with frosting cupcakes! It is strangely more difficult than it looks. We hope this step-by-step guide will help you achieve the perfect result.

1 To keep the consistency of the buttercream frosting as smooth as possible, beat the frosting with an electric hand beater before starting. Between frosting each cupcake, use a knife to stir the frosting.

2 Start by scooping up the most buttercream you can in one go with an offset spatula and place it in the center of the cupcake.

3 Keeping the spatula angled so that its flat side remains in contact with the buttercream, work the frosting out to one edge of the cupcake by gently pushing it using small strokes with the spatula (see top left).

4 Take another scoop of buttercream and repeat step 3, this time pushing the frosting out to the opposite edge of the cupcake (see top right).

5 Add one more scoop of frosting to the cupcake to bring the edges together, making a central peak with the remaining frosting (see bottom left).

6 Dip the end of the spatula into the center of the frosted cupcake and, in an counter-clockwise direction, drag the spatula in a circular motion to create a swirl effect (see bottom right).

7 Decorate the cupcake as desired. Make sure to put any sprinkles on to the cupcakes as quickly as possible, otherwise the frosting will set a little, making it hard for any decorations to stick.

step by step!

Vanilla Buttercream Frosting

This is our favorite and most traditional frosting recipe. Simple and unadorned, it lends itself perfectly to many of our cupcakes and layer cakes, but by all means tint it with a little color if you wish. We can't stress too much how the flavor and consistency are dependent on the quality of these simple ingredients, so don't buy anything but the best.

In a large mixing bowl beat the butter, milk, vanilla extract, and half the confectioners' sugar until smooth – this can take several minutes with an electric hand mixer. Gradually add the remainder of the confectioners' sugar and beat again until the buttercream is smooth and creamy.

If you want to color your buttercream, always start with one drop of coloring and beat thoroughly. This will be all you need to achieve a very pale pastel hue. Add carefully, drop by drop, and beat after each addition to build up to your desired shade.

Makes enough to frost
15–20 regular or about
60 mini cupcakes

8 tablespoons unsalted butter, at room temperature
¼ cup 2% reduced-fat milk, at room temperature
1 teaspoon pure vanilla extract
5 cups confectioners' sugar, sifted
Few drops of food coloring (optional)

Chocolate Buttercream Frosting

This makes a rich, velvety chocolate buttercream. It's irresistible; anything frosted with this one is always quickly devoured by adults and children alike. Use generously on cupcakes and layer cakes for the ultimate chocolate treat.

Break the chocolate into pieces and place in a microwave-safe bowl. Melt in the microwave on medium in 30-second intervals until smooth and of a thick pouring consistency. Stir well in between, to avoid burning the chocolate. Alternatively melt the chocolate in a heatproof bowl over a saucepan of barely simmering water. Stir occasionally until it has completely melted and is quite smooth. Leave to cool slightly.

In a large mixing bowl beat the butter, milk, vanilla, and confectioners' sugar until smooth – this can take several minutes with an electric hand mixer. Add the melted chocolate and beat again until thick and creamy. If it looks too runny to use when trying to frost cupcakes or cakes, simply keep beating – this will thicken the frosting and improve its consistency.

Makes enough to frost
15–20 regular or
60 mini cupcakes

6oz bittersweet chocolate (70% cocoa solids)
1 cup (2 sticks) unsalted butter, at room temperature
1 tablespoon 2% reduced-fat milk, at room temperature
1 teaspoon pure vanilla extract
2½ cups confectioners' sugar, sifted

Lemon Buttercream Frosting

This lemon buttercream perfectly complements our lemon cupcakes or layer cake – its citrus tang makes it the perfect foil for the sweet cake. It also smells delicious!

In a large mixing bowl beat the butter, 2 tablespoons lemon juice, lemon zest, and half the confectioners' sugar until smooth – this can take several minutes with an electric hand mixer. Gradually add the remainder of the confectioners' sugar and beat again until smooth and creamy. If needed, thin with additional lemon juice.

Use this frosting on the lemon cupcakes (see page 19) or inside and on top of the lemon layer cake (see page 134).

Makes enough to frost
15–20 regular cupcakes or
1 "two-layer" cake

**8 tablespoons unsalted butter,
  at room temperature**
**2–3 tablespoons freshly squeezed
  lemon juice**
**Grated zest of 1–2 unwaxed
  lemons (you need 2 teaspoons)**
**4¼ cups confectioners' sugar,
  sifted**

basic frostings

Coffee Buttercream Frosting

This is real coffee buttercream, with its full flavor coming from good espresso powder. Partnered with our chocolate cupcakes, it becomes a mocha hit.

Makes enough to frost
15–20 regular or about
60 mini cupcakes

**10 tablespoons unsalted butter,
at room temperature**
**1 tablespoon 2% reduced-fat
milk, at room temperature**
**2 teaspoons instant espresso
powder, dissolved in a small
amount of hot water, cooled**
**3¼ cups confectioners' sugar,
sifted**

In a large mixing bowl beat the butter, milk, espresso mixture, and half the confectioners' sugar until smooth – this can take several minutes with an electric hand mixer. Gradually add the remaining confectioners' sugar to produce a buttercream of a creamy and smooth consistency.

Orange Cream Cheese Frosting

Less sweet, but no less delicious than our traditional buttercream frostings, this fresh, creamy frosting is the natural choice for the carrot cupcakes but it would be a great one for the marmalade cupcakes, too (see page 44).

Place all the ingredients in a mixing bowl and beat well until thoroughly combined and the frosting is smooth and pale – this can take several minutes with an electric hand mixer.

Cream cheese frosting must be stored in the refrigerator, but it keeps well. Before re-using, allow it come to room temperature and then beat again.

Makes enough to frost 15–20 regular or about 60 mini cupcakes

6oz cream cheese, at room temperature
4¼ cups confectioners' sugar, sifted
9 tablespoons unsalted butter, at room temperature
Grated zest of 1 orange

Lime and Coconut Buttercream

For a more exotic flavor, this combination of fresh lime and coconut always satisfies. Great on vanilla cupcakes, but how about trying it with the ginger cupcakes (see page 83)?

Makes enough to frost
15–20 regular or about
60 mini cupcakes

8 tablespoons unsalted butter,
at room temperature
2–3 tablespoons freshly squeezed
lime juice
Grated zest of 1–2 limes (you
need 2 teaspoons)
5 cups confectioners' sugar,
sifted
Handful of desiccated coconut,
to decorate

In a large mixing bowl beat the butter, 2 tablespoons of lime juice, lime zest, and half the confectioners' sugar until smooth – this can take several minutes with an electric hand mixer. Gradually add the remainder of the confectioners' sugar and beat until thick and creamy. If needed, thin with additional lime juice.

Use this frosting on vanilla cupcakes and finish with a sprinkling of coconut. The frosting will set quickly, so make sure to put the coconut on at once.

tip

For a special occasion, you could even place fresh orchids on top of the cakes, as the beauty of these exotic flowers goes so well with these cupcakes.

Festive and Seasonal

On the following pages you'll find ideas for seasonal cupcakes and celebrations and special days throughout the year. Of course you don't have to reserve these cupcakes for the times and events of the year we have suggested, though some of the recipes are intended to celebrate fresh seasonal ingredients, such as strawberries in the summer months and cranberries around Christmas time. And by all means deviate from our suggested decorations for these cupcakes to suit your particular occasion. You don't have to decorate them at all; they'll still be a treat, any day of the week!

The preparation of some of these cupcakes and frostings is a step beyond the basic recipes of the preceding chapters, but they can be made by almost anyone and enjoyed by all. Just don't forget the importance of good-quality ingredients, and patience.

Honey and Granola Cupcakes

As the New Year begins, it feels good to shake off a little of the over-indulgence of the holidays. It feels good too to produce something made in your own kitchen, especially using the wholesome ingredients that go into this recipe. Besides being an all-day energy-boosting treat, they are completely satisfying and delicious warmed for breakfast, simply served plain, spread with honey and butter, or topped with cream cheese frosting.

Makes about
14 regular cupcakes

8 tablespoons unsalted butter,
    at room temperature
½ cup packed light brown sugar
½ cup mild honey
2 large eggs, free-range or organic
1⅔ cups all-purpose flour
½ teaspoon baking soda
½ teaspoon baking powder
½ teaspoon salt
¼ cup 2% reduced-fat milk,
    at room temperature
½ teaspoon pure vanilla extract
¼ cup low-fat plain yogurt
2½ cups granola (pick out any
    large whole nuts if you can)

Preheat the oven to 350°F and line 14 cups in two 12-cup muffin pans with cupcake liners.

In a large mixing bowl cream the butter, brown sugar, and honey until the mixture is light and fluffy, which should take about 2–3 minutes using an electric hand mixer. Add the eggs, one at a time, mixing for a few minutes after each addition.

Sift the flour, baking soda, baking powder, and salt together into a separate bowl. Mix the milk, vanilla, and yogurt together. Add one-third of the flour mixture to the creamed mixture and beat well. Pour in one-third of the milk mixture and beat again. Repeat these steps until all the flour and milk have been added. Fold in the granola carefully to incorporate evenly.

Carefully spoon the mixture into the cups, filling them about two-thirds full. Bake in the oven for about 25 minutes until golden brown. To check they are cooked, insert a wooden skewer in the center of one of the cupcakes – it should come out clean.

Remove from the oven and leave the cupcakes in their pans for about 10 minutes. Serve warm with butter and honey or with a little cream cheese frosting (see page 35) made without the orange zest.

Blueberry and Cornmeal Cupcakes

Somewhere between a cupcake and a muffin, this recipe works perfectly for breakfast or makes a healthier snack during the day or at teatime. The use of cornmeal gives a satisfying crunchy texture, coupled with the delicious taste and color of the blueberries.

Preheat the oven to 350°F and line 14 cups in two 12-cup muffin pans with cupcake liners.

In a large mixing bowl cream the butter and sugars until pale and smooth, which should take 3–5 minutes using an electric hand mixer. Add the eggs, one at a time, mixing for a few minutes after each addition.

Sift the flour, cornmeal, baking soda, baking powder, and salt together into a separate bowl. Add one-third of the flour mixture to the creamed mixture and beat until just combined. Add half of the buttermilk and mix until just combined. Repeat these steps until all the flour and buttermilk have been added. Gently fold in the blueberries.

Carefully spoon the mixture into the cups, filling them about two-thirds full. Bake in the oven for about 25 minutes until slightly raised and golden brown. To check they are cooked, insert a wooden skewer in the center of one of the cupcakes – it should come out clean.

Remove from the oven and leave the cupcakes in their pans for about 10 minutes. These are delicious served still warm, maybe with some butter and a few fresh blueberries. You could dust the tops of the cupcakes with a little confectioners' sugar before serving.

Makes about
14 regular cupcakes

**8 tablespoons unsalted butter,
at room temperature**
⅔ cup demerara sugar
½ cup packed light brown sugar
2 large eggs, free-range or organic
**1 cup plus 3 tablespoons
all-purpose flour**
1 scant cup yellow cornmeal
½ teaspoon baking soda
½ teaspoon baking powder
½ teaspoon salt
½ cup buttermilk
**1 cup blueberries, fresh or frozen,
at room temperature**
**Confectioners' sugar, for dusting
(optional)**

tip

To prevent the blueberries from sinking in the cupcakes, toss them gently in a little all-purpose flour before folding them into the batter.

Frances' Pecan and Orange Marmalade Cupcakes

These delicious cupcakes were devised by one of our chefs, Frances Money, as a great breakfast food, particularly during the New Year winter months after Christmas, when we are all trying to be a bit more healthy after all the rich festive food. A great start to the day, especially served straight from the oven and maybe even with a bit more marmalade on the side!

Makes about
14 regular cupcakes

4 tablespoons unsalted butter, melted and cooled
½ cup corn oil
¼ cup orange juice (juice of approx. 1 small orange)
Grated zest of 1 small orange
3 tablespoons thick-cut orange marmalade
¼ teaspoon pure vanilla extract
1⅔ cups all-purpose flour
1 teaspoon baking soda
½ teaspoon salt
2 large eggs, free-range or organic
¾ cup sugar, preferably golden bakers'
¾ cup pecans, toasted in a 350°F oven for 10 minutes, chopped

To decorate
Extra orange marmalade (slightly warmed if difficult to spread)
Toasted pecans, chopped (optional)

Preheat the oven to 350°F and line 14 cups in two 12-cup muffin pans with cupcake liners.

In a large mixing bowl combine the butter, corn oil, orange juice, orange zest, marmalade, and vanilla. Set aside.

In a separate bowl, sift the flour, baking soda, and salt together and set aside. Beat the eggs and sugar in a large bowl with an electric hand mixer, until the mixture is light, fluffy, and quite thick. Slowly add the butter, oil, and juice mixture, keeping the beater on a low speed, until it is all combined.

Add one-third of the flour mixture to the combined egg, sugar, and oil mixture and beat until just combined. Pour in another third of the flour and beat again. Repeat with the last third of flour and beat until the batter just comes together. Gently fold in the pecans.

Carefully spoon the mixture evenly into the cups, filling each one about two-thirds full. Bake in the oven for about 25 minutes, until slightly raised and golden brown. To check they are cooked, insert a wooden skewer in the center of one of the cupcakes – it should come out clean.

Remove from the oven and while the cupcakes are still warm, top each one with 1 teaspoon marmalade and spread all over the top. Sprinkle with extra pecans, if you wish. Serve immediately if possible!

Rose Cupcakes

Adorned with pale pink rose buttercream and sugared – or even fresh – rose petals, these delicately scented cupcakes are sure to inspire romance. A perfect gift for loved ones on Valentine's Day.

Makes 12 regular cupcakes

8 tablespoons unsalted butter, at room temperature
1 cup plus 2 tablespoons sugar, preferably golden bakers'
2 large eggs, free-range or organic
1 cup self-rising flour
¾ cup plus 1 tablespoon all-purpose flour
½ teaspoon rosewater (available at specialty food stores), or to taste
½ cup 2% reduced-fat milk, at room temperature

To decorate
1 batch of Rose Buttercream Frosting (see page 49)
Crystallized rose petals or other Valentine-themed decorations

Preheat the oven to 350°F and line a 12-cup muffin pan with cupcake liners.

In a large mixing bowl cream the butter and sugar until the mixture is pale and smooth, which should take 3–5 minutes using an electric hand mixer. Add the eggs, one at a time, mixing for a few minutes after each addition.

Sift the two flours together into a separate bowl. Mix a little of the rosewater with the milk and test it: rosewater varies in quality and strength, so taste the mixture and adjust the amount you add accordingly. Add one-third of the flours to the creamed mixture and beat well. Pour in one-third of the milk and beat again. Repeat these steps until all the flour and milk have been added.

Carefully spoon the mixture into the cups, filling them about two-thirds full. Bake in the oven for about 25 minutes until slightly raised and golden brown. To check they are cooked, insert a wooden skewer in the center of one of the cupcakes – it should come out clean.

Remove from the oven and leave the cupcakes in the pan for about 10 minutes before carefully placing on a wire rack to cool. Once they are completely cool, frost with rose buttercream and sprinkle with your choice of decorations – crystallized rose petals, sugar hearts, sugar flowers, sprinkles – it's up to you!

Rose Buttercream Frosting

This buttercream, infused with rosewater, is simply adapted from our classic vanilla buttercream. By adding the rosewater carefully you can produce a subtle or stronger flavor, depending on your preference. Perfect on our rose cupcakes (see page 46), this frosting could also be used on vanilla (see page 15) or orange cupcakes (see page 52).

In a large mixing bowl beat the butter, milk, vanilla, and half the confectioners' sugar until smooth – this can take several minutes using an electric hand mixer. Gradually add the remainder of the confectioners' sugar and beat again until the buttercream is smooth and creamy. Add the rosewater at the very end and beat thoroughly, tasting to check if it is flavored enough.

To color, simply beat in a tiny drop of pink food coloring.

Makes enough to frost 15–20 regular or 60 mini cupcakes

8 tablespoons unsalted butter,
    at room temperature
¼ cup 2% reduced-fat milk,
    at room temperature
1 teaspoon pure vanilla extract
5 cups confectioners' sugar, sifted
½ teaspoon rosewater, or to taste
Pink food coloring (optional)

Chocolate Liqueur Cupcakes

As an alternative to the more delicate rose cupcakes, these rich chocolate truffle and liqueur cupcakes make an indulgent Valentine's present. We have suggested champagne truffles to decorate but almost any variety of truffle would work equally well.

Make the chocolate cupcakes in the usual way, but use only ⅓ cup plus 1 tablespoon milk and mix with the framboise.

When the cupcakes are completely cool, frost them with the chocolate buttercream frosting, then place a champagne truffle in the center of each one. Press down gently so that the truffle does not roll off.

Makes 16 regular cupcakes

**1 batch of Chocolate Cupcakes
   (see page 16)**
**2 tablespoons framboise
   (raspberry eau-de-vie)**

To decorate
**1 batch of Chocolate Buttercream
   Frosting (see page 29)**
16 champagne truffles

Orange Cupcakes

You could make these cupcakes for an afternoon tea on Mother's Day. Serve them on pretty vintage china with fresh spring flowers and maybe a cup of fragranced tea, such as jasmine or lapsang souchong.

Makes 12 regular cupcakes

8 tablespoons unsalted butter, at room temperature
1 cup plus 2 tablespoons sugar, preferably golden bakers'
2 large eggs, free-range or organic
1 cup self-rising flour
¾ cup plus 1 tablespoon all-purpose flour
⅓ cup plus 1 tablespoon 2% reduced-fat milk, at room temperature
2 tablespoons freshly squeezed orange juice
Grated zest of 1 orange (you need 1 teaspoon)

To decorate
1 batch of Orange Blossom Buttercream Frosting (see opposite)
Orange sugar flowers, candied orange zest, or fresh orange blossoms

Preheat the oven to 350°F and line a 12-cup muffin pan with cupcake liners.

In a large mixing bowl cream the butter and sugar until the mixture is pale and smooth, which should take 3–5 minutes using an electric hand mixer Add the eggs, one at a time, mixing for a few minutes after each addition.

Sift the two flours together into a separate bowl. Add one-third of the flours to the creamed mixture and beat well. Pour in half the milk and beat well. Add another third of the flour and beat again. Beat in the remainder of the milk and all the orange juice. Finish by adding the last third of the flour and the orange zest and beat well. If the mixture looks like it is curdling slightly, don't panic – simply add another spoonful of all-purpose flour and beat well.

Carefully spoon the mixture into the cups, filling them about two-thirds full. Bake in the oven for about 25 minutes until lightly golden brown. To check they are cooked, insert a wooden skewer in the center of one of the cupcakes – it should come out clean.

Remove from the oven and leave the cupcakes in the pan for about 10 minutes before carefully placing on a wire rack to cool. Once they are completely cool, frost with orange blossom buttercream frosting and decorate with either an orange sugar flower, orange zest or, if you are lucky enough to find any, some fresh orange blossom flowers.

Orange Blossom Buttercream Frosting

In a large mixing bowl beat the butter, juice, and half the confectioners' sugar until smooth – this can take several minutes using an electric hand mixer. Gradually add the remaining confectioners' sugar and beat until smooth and creamy. Add the orange blossom water and beat again. Taste the frosting to see if it is flavored enough and if necessary add a little more of the orange blossom water.

Makes enough to frost
12–15 regular cupcakes

8 tablespoons unsalted butter, at room temperature
2 tablespoons freshly squeezed orange juice
4½ cups confectioners' sugar, sifted
1–2 teaspoons orange blossom water (available at specialty food stores)

Earl Grey Cupcakes

The delicate bergamot citrus flavor of Earl Grey tea will intensify with every bite here. If you are a tea lover and have a fondness for a particular blend, you could easily substitute that one. We think these cupcakes make an ideal Mother's Day treat as they look so pretty piled on a plate at the center of a special afternoon tea.

**Makes about
12 regular cupcakes**

½ cup 2% reduced-fat milk,
    at room temperature
4 Earl Grey teabags
**8 tablespoons unsalted butter,
    at room temperature**
**1 cup plus 2 tablespoons
    granulated sugar**
½ **teaspoon almond extract
    (optional)**
2 large eggs, free-range or organic
¾ **cup plus 2 tablespoons
    self-rising flour**
¾ **cup all-purpose flour**

To decorate (optional)
**1 batch of Vanilla Buttercream
    Frosting (see page 26),
    colored lilac**
**Granulated sugar or
    sugar flowers**

Preheat the oven to 350°F and line a 12-cup muffin pan with cupcake liners.

Heat the milk in a saucepan over medium heat until it just begins to boil. Remove from the heat and add the teabags. Cover and leave to infuse for about 30 minutes, then discard the teabags.

In a large mixing bowl cream the butter and sugar until the mixture is pale and smooth, which should take 3–5 minutes using an electric hand mixer. Add the almond extract, if using, and the eggs, one at a time, mixing for a few minutes after each addition.

Sift the two flours together into a separate bowl. Add one-third of the flours to the creamed mixture and beat well. Pour in one-third of the infused milk and beat again. Repeat these steps until all the flour and milk have been added.

Carefully spoon the mixture into the cups, filling them about two-thirds full. Bake in the oven for about 25 minutes until slightly raised and golden brown. To check they are cooked, insert a wooden skewer in the center of one of the cupcakes – it should come out clean.

Remove from the oven and leave the cupcakes in the pan for about 10 minutes before carefully placing on a wire rack to cool. Once they are completely cool, you could frost the cupcakes with lilac-colored vanilla buttercream and sprinkle with a little extra granulated sugar and sugar flowers.

Coffee Cupcakes

You will find no coffee extract here – these are the real deal with a full kick of espresso powder. They make a delicious Mother's Day gift or, in mini size, an after-dinner treat. Topped with crushed walnuts or chocolate-covered espresso beans, these are cupcakes for grown-ups.

Preheat the oven to 350°F and line a 12-cup muffin pan or three 12-cup mini muffin pans with cupcake liners.

In a large mixing bowl cream the butter and sugars until the mixture is pale and smooth, which should take 3–5 minutes using an electric hand mixer. Add the eggs, one at a time, mixing for a few minutes after each addition. Do not worry if the mixture curdles a bit after adding the eggs – this will not affect the outcome.

Sift the flours together into a separate bowl. Whisk the vanilla extract and espresso powder with the milk. Add one-third of the flours to the creamed mixture and beat well. Pour in one-third of the milk and beat again. Repeat these steps until all the flour and milk have been added.

Carefully spoon the mixture into the cups, filling them about two-thirds full. Bake in the oven for about 25 minutes (regular size) or 15 minutes (mini size) until slightly raised and golden brown. To check they are cooked, insert a wooden skewer in the center of one of the cupcakes – it should come out clean.

Remove from the oven and leave the cupcakes in the pan for about 10 minutes before carefully placing on a wire rack to cool.

Once they are completely cool, frost with coffee buttercream and decorate with either whole or crushed walnuts or chocolate-covered espresso beans.

Makes 12 regular or
36 mini cupcakes

8 tablespoons unsalted butter,
    at room temperature
⅔ cup demerara sugar
½ cup packed light brown sugar
2 large eggs, free-range or organic
¾ cup plus 2 tablespoons
    self-rising flour
¾ cup all-purpose flour
¼ teaspoon pure vanilla extract
1 tablespoon instant
    espresso powder
½ cup 2% reduced-fat milk,
    at room temperature

To decorate
1 batch of Coffee Buttercream
    Frosting (see page 32)
Walnuts or chocolate-covered
    espresso beans

Milky Way Cupcakes

These are an extremely rich Easter treat, hugely popular with adults and children alike. They are not really cupcakes, but are incredibly easy to make and look great with Easter decorations. It is surprisingly hard to resist eating more than one!

Makes about 10 regular or
30 mini cupcakes

**2 tablespooons unsalted butter,
    at room temperature**
2 tablespoons light corn syrup
**9oz Milky Way bars,
    chopped into ½-inch cubes**
6½ cups corn flakes

To decorate
**1 batch of Chocolate Buttercream
    Frosting (see page 29)**
**Easter chicks or rabbits or small
    chocolate eggs**

Line a 12-cup muffin pan or three 12-cup mini muffin pans with cupcake liners.

Melt the butter and corn syrup in a saucepan over very low heat, stirring constantly. Add the chopped candy bars and keep stirring until just melted. Remove from the heat and gently fold in the corn flakes completely – although don't mix too forcefully or you will crush the corn flakes.

Press a spoonful of the mixture loosely into each cupcake liner and leave them to cool and set. When they are completely cool, put a small amount of chocolate buttercream frosting in the center of each cupcake and decorate with an Easter chick or rabbit or a small chocolate egg.

Should there be any uneaten, the cupcakes can be stored in an airtight container for about 3 days.

Caramel Cupcakes

An equally rich alternative to our other Easter cupcakes, these would also be delicious on a cold winter's day and, once frosted with our caramel buttercream frosting, could be decorated with almost any crunchy chocolate or toffee pieces.

Preheat the oven to 350°F and line a 12-cup muffin pan with cupcake liners. If making your own caramel sauce, make it first as it needs to cool before you use it.

In a large mixing bowl cream the butter and sugars until pale and smooth, which should take about 3–5 minutes using an electric hand mixer. Add the eggs, one at a time, mixing for a few minutes after each addition. Add the vanilla extract.

Sift the flours together into a separate bowl. Add one-third of the flour to the creamed mixture and mix until the batter just comes together. Add the caramel sauce and beat well. Add another third of the flour and beat until it just comes together. Add the cream and again beat well. Add the remaining flour and beat until the mixture is combined.

Carefully spoon the mixture into the cups, filling them about two-thirds full. Bake in the oven for about 25 minutes until slightly raised and golden brown. To check they are cooked, insert a wooden skewer in the center of one of the cupcakes – it should come out clean.

Remove from the oven and leave the cupcakes in the pan for about 10 minutes before carefully placing on a wire rack to cool.

Once they are completely cool, frost with caramel buttercream frosting. Immediately sprinkle the chocolate-covered toffee over the cupcakes.

Makes 12 regular cupcakes

8 tablespoons unsalted butter, at room temperature
⅔ cup packed light brown sugar
⅔ cup packed dark brown sugar
2 large eggs, free-range or organic
½ teaspoon pure vanilla extract
¾ cup plus 2 tablespoons self-rising flour
¾ cup all-purpose flour
1 teaspoon baking soda
¼ teaspoon salt
⅓ cup Caramel Sauce (see page 64)
¼ cup heavy cream

To decorate
1 batch of Caramel Buttercream Frosting (see page 65)
¼ cup coarsely chopped chocolate-covered toffee

Caramel Sauce

This makes about ¾ cup – plenty to use in the caramel cupcakes (see page 63).

1¼ cups sugar, preferably golden bakers'
⅔ cup water

Put the sugar and ⅓ cup of water in a heavy saucepan and stir over low heat until the sugar has dissolved. Increase the heat and cook over a high heat for about 10 minutes, after which the mixture should be dark amber in color.

Remove the pan from the heat and leave to cool slightly. Stir gently to help it cool but take great care as the sugar is extremely hot – this might be best done by holding the pan away from you over a sink.

Once the mixture has cooled slightly, slowly add the remaining ⅓ cup water to the mix and continue stirring. Again hold the pan away from you when adding the water as it may spatter.

When the sauce is completely cool, pour into a bowl and cover until ready to use. Any unused sauce can be stored in an airtight container for up to a week.

Caramel Buttercream Frosting

This buttercream works well with the caramel cupcakes (see page 63) or the chocolate cupcakes (see page 16), although it will take slightly more patience and care than others. Pay particular attention not to burn yourself but it is well worth the effort and we highly recommend it!

Place the butter, milk, and brown sugar in a heavy saucepan over high heat and stir to combine. Bring to a boil, stirring continuously, and allow it to boil for 1 minute.

Remove from the heat and whisk in half of the confectioners' sugar. Leave the mixture to cool slightly, then add the remaining confectioners' sugar and the vanilla extract and stir until it thickens to the desired consistency.

This frosting is best used immediately as it sets quickly. If making in advance, or using any left over, thin it with a little heavy cream and beat well before using. Alternatively, heat the frosting for 10 seconds in a microwave.

Makes enough to frost
12 regular cupcakes

**4 tablespoons unsalted butter,
    at room temperature**
**6 tablespoons milk, at room
    temperature**
1 cup packed light brown sugar
**2⅓ cups confectioners' sugar,
    sifted**
½ teaspoon pure vanilla extract
Heavy cream, as needed

Malted Cupcakes

These malt-flavored cupcakes are perfect for children to help bake, give, and then share with their dads come Father's Day. Top with marshmallow frosting or chocolate buttercream. Exceedingly tasty, with a pinch of nostalgia!

Makes 12 regular cupcakes

8 tablespoons unsalted butter,
    at room temperature
½ cup packed light brown sugar
½ cup sugar, preferably
    golden bakers'
2 large eggs, free-range or organic
¾ cup plus 2 tablespoons
    self-rising flour
⅓ cup plus 1 tablespoon
    all-purpose flour
7 tablespoons chocolate malted
    milk powder, preferably
    Ovaltine
½ cup 2% reduced-fat milk,
    at room temperature
½ teaspoon pure vanilla extract
1 tablespoon sour cream

To decorate
1 batch of Marshmallow Frosting
    (see page 69) or Chocolate
    Buttercream Frosting (see
    page 29)
Chocolate-covered malted milk
    balls or extra chocolate malted
    milk powder

Preheat the oven to 350°F and line a 12-cup muffin pan with cupcake liners.

In a large mixing bowl cream the butter and sugars until pale and smooth, which should take about 3–5 minutes using an electric hand mixer. Add the eggs, one at a time, mixing for a few minutes after each addition.

Sift the flours and chocolate malted milk powder into a separate bowl. Mix the milk, vanilla extract, and sour cream together. Add one-third of the flour mixture to the creamed mixture and beat well. Pour in one-third of the milk and beat again. Repeat these steps until all the flour mixture and milk have been added.

Carefully spoon the mixture into the cups, filling them about two-thirds full. Bake in the oven for about 25 minutes until slightly raised and golden brown. To check they are cooked, insert a wooden skewer in the center of one of the cupcakes – it should come out clean.

Remove from the oven and leave the cupcakes in the pan for about 10 minutes before carefully placing on a wire rack to cool.

Once they are completely cool, frost these cupcakes with chocolate buttercream or marshmallow frosting and decorate with whole or crushed chocolate-covered malted milk balls or a simple sprinkling of chocolate malted milk powder. For a lucky father, you could use some sugar lettering to spell out "Daddy" on one of them or write it using an frosting tube or pen available in many colors in supermarkets.

Marshmallow Frosting

Please note that this frosting is easiest to work with while it is still slightly warm, so use it immediately. As it has a very sticky consistency, you may find it a little harder to frost with than most of our frostings, but be patient and persevere! Any left over can be kept in the refrigerator overnight, but we would not recommend keeping it any longer.

Cook the sugar, corn syrup, and water in a saucepan over high heat until the mixture reaches the soft-ball stage (239°F) on a sugar thermometer, which should take about 6 minutes. Remove from the heat.

Meanwhile, in a clean bowl beat the egg whites with an electric hand mixer until soft peaks start to form. With the blades still beating on a low speed, slowly pour the hot sugar syrup in a steady stream on to the egg whites. Continue to beat on low speed until all the hot syrup has been added.

Increase the speed to medium-high and continue beating the mixture until it becomes thick, glossy and cool. Add the vanilla extract towards the end of the mixing process.

Makes enough to frost 12 regular cupcakes with some left over

⅔ cup granulated sugar
Scant ¼ cup light corn syrup
1½ tablespoons water
2 large egg whites, free-range
  or organic
½ teaspoon pure vanilla extract

Peanut Butter Cupcakes

This is a fairly dense and rich cupcake. However, a batch is too good to make only for July 4th! Any kind of peanut butter candy will work for decoration – peanut butter chips, chopped peanut butter cups, Reese's pieces, or whatever else you fancy.

Makes 12 regular cupcakes

5 tablespoons unsalted butter,
    at room temperature
⅔ cup smooth peanut butter
1 cup packed dark brown sugar
2 large eggs, free-range or organic
1 teaspoon pure vanilla extract
¾ cup plus 1 tablepoon
    all-purpose flour, sifted
1 teaspoon baking powder
Pinch of salt
¼ cup 2% reduced-fat milk,
    at room temperature

To decorate
1 batch of Milk Chocolate
    Frosting (see page 72)
Peanut butter or milk
    chocolate chips

Preheat the oven to 350°F and line a 12-cup muffin pan with cupcake liners.

In a large mixing bowl cream the butter, peanut butter, and sugar until well blended. Add the eggs, one at a time, mixing for a few minutes after each addition, and then stir in the vanilla extract.

Combine the flour, baking powder, and salt in a separate bowl. Add one-third of the flour to the creamed mixture and beat well. Pour in one-third of the milk and beat again. Repeat these steps until all the flour mixture and milk have been added.

Carefully spoon the mixture into the cups, filling them about two-thirds full. Bake in the oven for about 20 minutes until slightly raised and golden brown. To check they are cooked, insert a wooden skewer in the center of one of the cupcakes – it should come out clean.

Remove from the oven and leave the cupcakes in the pan for about 10 minutes before carefully placing on a wire rack to cool.

Once they are completely cool, frost with milk chocolate frosting. Top with peanut butter chips or milk chocolate chips, and don't forget your American flag if it's Independence Day.

Milk Chocolate Frosting

We use this frosting specifically for our peanut butter cupcakes (see page 70) as we think it works better than our buttercream frosting and sometimes makes a nice change. It is considerably more fussy to make but tastes delicious! By all means try it out on some of the other cupcakes – vanilla or chocolate maybe?

Makes enough to frost
12 regular cupcakes

¼ cup heavy cream
2 tablespoons unsalted butter,
    at room temperature
10½ oz milk chocolate,
    broken into small pieces
½ teaspoon pure vanilla extract

Put the heavy cream and butter in a saucepan over very low heat. Stir constantly and do not let it come to a boil or it will burn. As soon as the butter has completely melted, remove from the heat and add the chocolate. Allow the chocolate to stand in the pan until softened, about 3 minutes. Add the vanilla extract and whisk until smooth.

Let the frosting stand at room temperature until it is cool and thick enough to spread on your cupcakes. Any unused frosting should be stored in a container in the refrigerator.

Strawberries and Cream Cupcakes

Primrose Bakery always uses seasonal fruit. So when summer is upon us, these are the cupcakes, preferably made with the sweetest and juiciest English strawberries, that fill our counters. This recipe is easiest made in a food processor, but you can still make it with an electric hand mixer.

Preheat the oven to 350°F and line 15 cups in two 12-cup muffin pans with cupcake liners.

Put the sugar, flour, baking powder, cornstarch, and puréed strawberries into a food processor. Pulse until evenly mixed (roughly 4 seconds). Add the butter and eggs and process briefly until even (roughly 10 seconds). If you are using an electric hand mixer, cream the butter and sugar together first, beat in the eggs, one by one, and then add the remaining ingredients and beat well together.

Carefully spoon the mixture into the cups, filling them about two-thirds full. Bake in the oven for about 25 minutes. The cupcakes will be fairly moist even when cooked.

Remove from the oven and leave the cupcakes in the pans for about 10 minutes before carefully placing on a wire rack to cool.

Once they are completely cool, carefully make a small hole in the center of each cupcake and use a teaspoon to fill the hole with strawberry jam – you can slightly warm the jam in a saucepan first to soften it.

Wash the 12 strawberries and pat dry with paper towels to limit any excess water and juice spoiling the buttercream once they are on the cupcakes. Decorate the cupcakes with vanilla buttercream frosting and, just before serving, place a fresh strawberry in the center of each cupcake.

Makes 15 regular cupcakes

1 cup plus 2 tablespoons granulated sugar
1⅓ cups self-rising flour, sifted
1 teaspoon baking powder
3 tablespoons cornstarch
½ cup coarsely puréed ripe strawberries
1 cup (2 sticks) unsalted butter, at room temperature
4 large eggs, free-range or organic

To decorate
Strawberry jam (1 teaspoon for each cupcake)
1 batch of Vanilla Buttercream Frosting (see page 26)
12 small strawberries

Coconut Cupcakes with Pink Vanilla Buttercream

If coconut desserts are your thing, these are going to be your ideal cupcake. Filled with moist coconut, encased in vanilla cake, topped with a delicate pink frosting and coconut shavings …a sweet treat in cupcake form.

Makes 12 regular cupcakes

8 tablespoons unsalted butter,
  at room temperature
¾ cup plus 1 tablespoon
  granulated sugar
2 large eggs, free-range or organic
½ teaspoon pure vanilla extract
⅛ teaspoon almond extract
  (optional)
¾ cup plus 2 tablespoons
  self-rising flour
¾ cup plus 1 tablespoon
  all-purpose flour
½ cup canned coconut milk
⅓ cup desiccated coconut

To decorate
1 batch of Vanilla Buttercream
  Frosting (see page 26),
  colored pale pink
Coconut flakes, lightly toasted in
  the oven for a few minutes

Preheat the oven to 350°F and line a 12-cup muffin pan with cupcake liners.

In a large mixing bowl cream the butter and sugar until pale and smooth, which should take about 3–5 minutes using an electric hand mixer. Add the eggs, one at a time, mixing for a few minutes after each addition and adding the vanilla and almond extract (if using) at the end.

Sift the two flours together into a separate bowl. Add one-third of the flours to the creamed mixture and beat well. Pour in one-third of the coconut milk and beat again. Repeat these steps until all the flour and milk have been added. Fold in the desiccated coconut using a metal spoon.

Carefully spoon the mixture into the cups, filling them about two-thirds full. Bake in the oven for about 25 minutes until slightly raised and golden brown. To check they are cooked, insert a wooden skewer in the center of one of the cupcakes – it should come out clean.

Remove from the oven and leave the cupcakes in the pan for about 10 minutes before carefully placing on a wire rack to cool.

Once they are completely cool, top the cupcakes with pink-tinted vanilla buttercream and sprinkle a few toasted coconut flakes over each one.

Raspberry Cupcakes

A perfect summer combination: fresh, tart raspberries and sweet, creamy white chocolate buttercream. Putting the raspberry jam directly into the cake once it's cooked makes the cupcakes look very pretty when cut open and the combination of tastes is divine. You could decorate them with some whole raspberries and serve with iced tea or fresh lemonade at a picnic or afternoon tea.

Preheat the oven to 350°F and line a 12-cup muffin pan with cupcake liners.

In a large mixing bowl cream the butter and sugar until pale and smooth, which should take about 3–5 minutes using an electric beater. Add the eggs, one at a time, mixing for a few minutes after each addition.

Sift the two flours together into a separate bowl. Mix the milk and vanilla extract together. Add one-third of the flours to the creamed mixture and beat well. Pour in one-third of the milk and beat again. Repeat these steps until all the flour and milk have been added.

Gently fold in the raspberry jam until most of it is combined. The idea is to have some jam streaks running through the mixture, rather than an evenly colored batter. Carefully spoon the batter into the cups, filling them about two-thirds full. Bake in the oven for about 25 minutes until slightly raised and golden brown.

Remove from the oven and leave the cupcakes in the pan for about 10 minutes before carefully placing on a wire rack to cool. Once they have cooled, cut a small hole in the center of each cupcake using a sharp knife or teaspoon and carefully place a teaspoon of jam inside – you can slightly warm the jam in a saucepan first to soften it before pushing it into the cake.

Top the cupcakes with white chocolate buttercream and decorate with fresh whole raspberries.

Makes 12 regular cupcakes

8 tablespoons unsalted butter,
    at room temperature
¾ cup plus 2 tablespoons
    granulated sugar
2 large eggs, free-range or organic
¾ cup plus 2 tablespoons
    self-rising flour
¾ cup plus 1 tablespoon
    all-purpose flour
½ cup 2% reduced-fat milk,
    at room temperature
1 teaspoon pure vanilla extract
3 tablespoons seedless
    raspberry jam

To decorate
Seedless raspberry jam
    (1 teaspoon for each cupcake)
1 batch of White Chocolate
    Buttercream Frosting
    (see page 80)
Fresh raspberries (2 for
    each cupcake)

White Chocolate Buttercream Frosting

This sweet white chocolate buttercream works brilliantly with the raspberry cupcakes (see page 79) but you could just as well add a swirl of it to the chocolate, strawberry, or coconut ones.

**Makes enough to frost
12 regular or 36 mini cupcakes**

**3½ oz high-quality white
   chocolate, broken into pieces
¼ cup Vanilla Buttercream
   Frosting (see page 26)
3 tablespoons heavy cream**

To melt the chocolate, put it in a microwave-safe bowl in the microwave on medium for 30 seconds, stir and then microwave in 30 second intervals – but be careful not to burn the chocolate. Alternatively, put the pieces in a heatproof bowl over a saucepan of barely simmering water. Stir occasionally until it has completely melted and is quite smooth. Leave to cool slightly.

Once the chocolate has cooled, combine all the ingredients and beat well until smooth and creamy. It is best to use this frosting immediately. If it begins to stiffen too much, soften with a little more cream or heat in the microwave for 10 seconds, beating well again before using.

This frosting needs to be refrigerated because it contains cream and will need to be beaten well again before use if it has become too cold and stiff.

Ginger Cupcakes

With the bite of ginger and molasses, these make great Halloween or winter treats. Be generous with ginger frosting to top the cakes and let your Halloween imagination go wild!

Preheat the oven to 350°F and line 18 cups in two 12-cup muffin pans with cupcake liners.

Melt the butter, sugar, and molasses in a saucepan over low heat. Cool briefly and then stir in the milk.

Add the chopped ginger to the beaten eggs and then beat into the butter mixture. Sift the flour, ground ginger, and salt and add to the warm mixture. Combine thoroughly.

Carefully spoon the mixture into the cups, filling them about two-thirds full. Bake in the oven for 30–35 minutes. To check they are cooked, insert a wooden skewer in the center of one of the cupcakes – it should come out clean.

Remove from the oven and leave the cupcakes in the pans for about 10 minutes before carefully placing on a wire rack to cool. Once they are completely cool, top each cake generously with ginger frosting then add your Halloween decorations – the scarier the better! Or you could simply top each one with a sprinkling of demerara sugar over the frosting.

These cupcakes are best eaten when they are freshly made; they tend to dry out a little more quickly than some of our other cupcakes.

Makes 18 regular cupcakes

14 tablespoons unsalted butter, diced, at room temperature
¾ cup packed dark brown sugar
3 tablespoons molasses
⅔ cup 2% reduced-fat milk, at room temperature
4 pieces of stem ginger, drained and chopped (reserve the syrup for the ginger fudge frosting)
2 large eggs, free-range or organic, beaten
2 cups self-rising flour
1 tablespoon ground ginger
Pinch of salt

To decorate
1 batch Ginger Frosting (see page 84)
Halloween decorations of your choice or demerara sugar

Ginger Frosting

This spicy frosting is the perfect creamy topping for the dark and dense ginger cupcakes (see page 83) – a really flavor-packed combination to devour behind closed doors or to hand out to trick-or-treaters.

Makes enough to frost
18 regular cupcakes

**9 tablespoons unsalted butter,
at room temperature**
**2 teaspoons freshly squeezed
lemon juice**
**4 tablespoons ginger syrup,
drained from a jar of
stem ginger**
**3 cups confectioners' sugar,
sifted**

In a large mixing bowl with an electric hand mixer, beat the butter for a few minutes until really smooth, then add the remaining ingredients and beat again until the frosting is smooth and creamy.

Pumpkin Cupcakes

Less sweet and a little spicier than some of our other cupcake recipes, these would work their magic before a night of trick-and-treating and the inevitable basket of sweets that comes home afterwards! If you can't find puréed pumpkin, cut a butternut squash into pieces, pare, de-seed, and steam for about 30 minutes. Then mash, pass through a sieve, and leave to drain for several hours to get rid of the excess water.

Makes 12 regular cupcakes

8 tablespoons unsalted butter, at room temperature
1⅓ cups packed light brown sugar
2 large eggs, free-range or organic
½ teaspoon pure vanilla extract
Scant ½ cup canned solid-pack pumpkin
¾ cup plus 2 tablespoons self-rising flour
¾ cup plus 1 tablespoon all-purpose flour
½ teaspoon ground cinnamon
½ teaspoon ground ginger
½ cup buttermilk (or ½ cup milk mixed with 1 teaspoon fresh lemon juice)

To decorate
1 batch of Spiced Cream Cheese Frosting (see page 87)
Ground cinnamon, grated nutmeg, or Halloween decorations of your choice

Preheat the oven to 350°F and line a 12-cup muffin pan with cupcake liners.

In a large mixing bowl cream the butter and sugar until the mixture is pale and smooth, which should take about 3–5 minutes using an electric hand mixer. Add the eggs, one at a time, and the vanilla extract, beating well after each addition. Add the pumpkin and beat until just combined.

Sift the flours, cinnamon, and ginger together into a bowl. Add one-third of the flours to the creamed mixture and beat until just combined. Add half of the buttermilk and beat again until just combined. Repeat these steps until all the flour and buttermilk have been added.

Carefully spoon the mixture into the cups, filling them about two-thirds full. Bake in the oven for about 25 minutes until slightly raised and golden brown. To check they are cooked, insert a wooden skewer in the center of one of the cakes – it should come out clean.

Remove from the oven and leave the cupcakes in the pan for about 10 minutes before placing carefully on a wire rack to cool.

Once they are completely cool, top the cupcakes with spiced cream cheese frosting and decorate with a sprinkling of cinnamon or nutmeg on the top or some Halloween decorations, if that's the occasion.

Spiced Cream Cheese Frosting

A simple variation on the orange cream cheese frosting from earlier in the book, this one could also work well with the carrot cupcakes (see page 21) but is especially delicious with the pumpkin cupcakes on a cold and windy Halloween night.

Place all the ingredients in a mixing bowl and beat well with an electric hand mixer until thoroughly combined and the frosting is smooth and pale.

This frosting must be stored in the refrigerator as it contains cream cheese, but will keep well. Before re-using, let it come to room temperature and then beat again.

Makes enough to frost
about 15 regular cupcakes

6oz cream cheese
4 cups confectioners' sugar,
sifted
8 tablespoons (1 stick) unsalted
butter, at room temperature
¼ teaspoon ground cinnamon
Pinch of ground cloves

Chocolate and Banana Cupcakes

A good recipe for a snack in front of the fire on a wet or chilly day. These cupcakes use our chocolate buttercream for their frosting, which really brings out the flavor of the chocolate chips in the cupcakes.

Makes 12 regular cupcakes

8 tablespoons (1 stick) unsalted
    butter, at room temperature
1¼ cups granulated sugar
2 eggs, free-range or organic,
    lightly beaten
1 teaspoon pure vanilla extract
1¾ cups plus 2 tablespoons
    all-purpose flour, sifted
2 teaspoons baking powder
4 ripe bananas, mashed
    with a fork
6oz bittersweet chocolate
    (70% cocoa solids), broken or
    chopped into small pieces

To decorate (optional)
1 batch of Chocolate Buttercream
    Frosting (see page 29)
Chopped walnuts

Preheat the oven to 350°F and line a 12-cup muffin pan with cupcake liners.

In a large mixing bowl cream the butter and sugar until the mixture is pale and smooth, which should take 3–5 minutes using an electric hand mixer. Add the eggs and vanilla extract and beat again briefly. Add the flour and baking powder and beat again until well combined. Stir in the mashed bananas and chocolate pieces using a wooden spoon.

Carefully spoon the mixture into the cups, filling them about two-thirds full. Bake in the oven for about 25 minutes. To check they are cooked, insert a wooden skewer in the center of one of the cupcakes – it should come out clean.

Remove from the oven and leave the cupcakes in the pan for about 10 minutes before carefully placing on a wire rack to cool.

Once they are completely cool, frost the cupcakes with chocolate buttercream. If you wish, pop some chopped walnuts on each one. Alternatively you could simply serve them with no frosting at all for a breakfast treat, warmed in the oven for a few minutes beforehand.

Chocolate-Orange Cupcakes

It is well established that the combination of orange and chocolate is a delectable union, so we have put this to good use with this cupcake recipe. The rich flavors of chocolate and seasonal ripe oranges make it a winter winner.

Preheat the oven to 350°F and line a 12-cup muffin pan with cupcake liners.

Break the chocolate into pieces and place in a microwave-safe bowl. Melt on medium in 30-second intervals until completely melted. Stir well between each session. Alternatively, place the chocolate in a heatproof bowl over a saucepan of barely simmering water. Stir occasionally until completely melted. Set the bowl aside to cool the chocolate.

In a large mixing bowl cream the butter, sugar, and orange zest until the mixture is pale and smooth, which should take 3–5 minutes using an electric hand mixer. Add the eggs and beat again briefly.

Combine the flour, baking soda, baking powder, and salt in a bowl. Mix the milk and orange juice together.

Add the chocolate to the creamed mixture and beat on a low speed until the mixture is just combined. The batter will still be streaky. Add one-third of the flour mix and beat until it all just comes together. Add half of the juice/milk mix and beat again until the mixture just comes together. Repeat these steps until all the ingredients have been incorporated.

Carefully spoon the mixture into the cups, filling them about two-thirds full. Bake in the oven for about 28–30 minutes. To check they are cooked, insert a wooden skewer in the center of one of the cupcakes – it should come out clean.

Remove from the oven and leave the cupcakes in the pan for about 10 minutes before carefully placing on a wire rack to cool. Once they are completely cool, frost the cupcakes with chocolate buttercream and decorate with a little orange zest or sugar flowers.

Makes 12 regular cupcakes

3½ oz bittersweet chocolate
(70% cocoa solids)
7 tablespoons unsalted butter,
at room temperature
¾ cup sugar, preferably
golden bakers'
Grated zest and juice of 1 orange
(you need ⅓ cup of juice)
2 large eggs, free-range or organic
1¼ cups all-purpose flour, sifted
½ teaspoon baking soda
½ teaspoon baking powder
½ teaspoon salt
1 tablespoon 2% reduced-fat
milk, at room temperature

To decorate
1 batch of Chocolate Buttercream
Frosting (see page 29)
Grated orange zest or
sugar flowers

Cranberry and Orange Cupcakes

These distinctively tangy cupcakes are delicious just baked and served warm, or try them topped with our orange blossom buttercream (see page 53) or orange cream cheese frosting (see page 35) as a healthier alternative to all the rich food during the Christmas period.

Makes 12 regular or
36 mini cupcakes

2 large eggs, free-range or organic
1 cup granulated sugar
6 tablespoons corn oil
½ cup plus 1 tablespoon
    sour cream
1 teaspoon pure vanilla extract
Grated zest of 1 orange (you
    need 1 teaspoon)
1½ cups all-purpose flour
½ teaspoon baking powder
¼ teaspoon baking soda
¼ teaspoon salt
1 teaspoon ground cinnamon
1 cup fresh or frozen
    cranberries, finely chopped

To decorate
1 batch of Orange Blossom
    Buttercream Frosting (see
    page 53) or Orange Cream
    Cheese Frosting (see page 35)
Whole fresh or dried cranberries
    or Christmas-themed
    decorations

Preheat the oven to 300°F and line a 12-cup muffin pan or three 12-cup mini muffin pans with cupcake liners.

In a large mixing bowl beat the eggs and sugar together until light and fluffy, which should take 3–5 minutes using an electric hand mixer. Slowly pour in the oil, a little at a time, beating well after each addition, then repeat the process with the sour cream and vanilla extract, making sure everything is well combined, and incorporate the orange zest at the end.

Sift the flour, baking powder, baking soda, salt, and cinnamon together in a bowl and then add to the batter and beat well. Finally, fold in the cranberries gently.

Carefully spoon the mixture into the cups, filling them about two-thirds full. Bake in the oven for about 25 minutes (regular size) or 15 minutes (mini size) until slightly raised and golden brown. To check they are cooked, insert a wooden skewer in the center of one of the cupcakes – it should come out clean.

Allow to cool in the pan for about 10 minutes before turning out on to a wire rack to cool. Once they are completely cool, frost with either orange blossom buttercream or orange cream cheese frosting and decorate with whole fresh or dried cranberries or some Christmas-themed decorations.

Peppermint Buttercream Frosting

As Christmas is upon us once again, this peppermint buttercream fits perfectly with the season's festivities. Team with chocolate cupcakes (see page 16) and top with crushed striped peppermint candies – the mint chocolate cupcakes will delight.

Makes enough to frost
15–20 regular or about
60 mini cupcakes

**8 tablespoons unsalted butter,
    at room temperature**
**¼ cup 2% reduced-fat milk,
    at room temperature**
**½ teaspoon pure peppermint
    extract (or more or less,
    depending on how minty
    you want your frosting)**
**5 cups confectioners' sugar,
    sifted**
**Few drops of green food coloring,
    as needed**

To decorate
**Chocolate chips, candy canes, or
    striped peppermint candies**

In a large mixing bowl beat the butter, milk, peppermint extract, and half the confectioners' sugar until smooth – this can take several minutes using an electric hand mixer. Gradually add the remainder of the confectioners' sugar and beat again until the buttercream is smooth and creamy. Taste the frosting at this stage to see if you want to add more peppermint extract.

Add a drop of green food coloring and beat thoroughly. This may be all you need to achieve a very pale pastel hue. Add carefully, drop by drop, and beat after each addition to build up to your desired shade.

Use the frosting to decorate chocolate cupcakes. Top with some chocolate chips or crush some candy canes or striped peppermint candies and sprinkle over each cupcake.

Brandy Buttercream Frosting

As an alternative to the traditional Christmas cake, brandy buttercream frosting could be used on either chocolate cupcakes or a chocolate layer cake. Either would be perfect served at a Christmas party with a glass of champagne.

In a large mixing bowl beat the butter, milk, brandy butter, vanilla extract, and half the confectioners' sugar until smooth – this can take a few minutes using an electric hand mixer. Gradually add the remainder of the confectioners' sugar until creamy and smooth.

Taste the buttercream to check if there is enough brandy butter, adding a little more if necessary, although remember how rich brandy butter is, especially combined with chocolate cake, so don't add too much!

Frost up a batch of chocolate cupcakes and then finish off with a brandy or cognac truffle or some pretty Christmas decoration.

The buttercream can be stored in an airtight container for up to 3 days at room temperature. Before re-using beat well.

Makes enough to frost
15–20 regular cupcakes

8 tablespoons unsalted butter,
at room temperature
¼ cup 2% reduced-fat milk,
at room temperature
2–3 tablespoons brandy butter
(available at specialty stores)
1 teaspoon pure vanilla extract
5 cups confectioners' sugar,
sifted

To decorate
Cognac or Brandy truffles

tip

If you decide to use this frosting on a chocolate layer cake (see page 128), it might work better if it were used in the middle layer only and then the cake were topped with chocolate buttercream (see page 29). You could decorate the cake with some truffles around the edge (you would need 10 or 12 for an 8-inch cake).

Special Occasions

Here are suggestions that show you our ideas for assembly and presentation based on the knowledge we have gained from the numerous cupcakes we have made over the past five years for birthdays, anniversaries, events, and gatherings. This is where cupcakes come into their own as they can be made and decorated to celebrate virtually any special occasion. You can batch them up to suit your situation, from a few for a child's birthday to several hundred for a large christening or anniversary party. Always be on the look out for imaginative, preferably edible, decorations, either in sugar or plastic (but remember to warn guests not to eat the plastic ones, especially children!), which can be stored and used when the occasion arises.

Sweetie Cupcakes

Sweetie cupcakes are of course going to attract and delight many a child. Our own children request them over and over again for special occasions, with the added bonus that they can participate in the decorating process.

Makes 12 regular cupcakes

1 batch of Vanilla or Chocolate Cupcakes (see page 15 or 16), regular size
1 batch of Chocolate Buttercream Frosting (see page 29)
An assortment of multicolored sweets, particularly the child's favorites, and/or big soft marshmallows, colored M&Ms, gummy worms, chocolate-covered malted milk balls, and candy necklaces

Make the cupcakes and frost with the chocolate buttercream. You could use vanilla buttercream, but with that one you need to put the sweets on fast before the frosting sets, which is why we recommend the chocolate as it takes longer to firm up, giving you more time to decide on which sweets to use and to help if a child is involved in the decorating.

A mixture of different shapes, sizes, and colors of sweet will enable you to build them up on top of the frosting to create a visual delight. It is always better to use too many than too few and pile them on without hesitation – this is not the recipe to use if worried about sugar content!

Birthday Cupcakes

You could use almost any of our cupcake flavors to make up a beautiful plate of birthday cupcakes. We have suggested vanilla cupcakes, but of course the birthday girl or boy may have a favorite flavor. You can buy some great packs of sugar lettering from most supermarkets to spell out your message, and be as extravagant as you like with decorations and candles. These days it's pretty easy to find an amazing choice of candles in all shapes and sizes to complement the chosen colors and themes of your birthday cupcakes.

Before you start to frost the cupcakes, decide on your decorations and message. We would suggest spreading "Happy Birthday" and the person's name over four regular-size cupcakes or putting one letter per mini cupcake and using as many as you need to spell out your message.

Press the letters onto the cupcakes as soon as you have frosted them, trying to keep them in the center of each cake. Mini cupcakes look really special if you put sprinkles around each letter, then lay the cupcakes out on a large plate or tray to spell out your message. You can do the same if using the lettering on four regular-size cupcakes, reserving any other decorations and some candles for the remaining cupcakes.

Makes 12 regular or
36 mini cupcakes

1 batch of Vanilla Cupcakes (see page 15), regular or mini size
1 batch of Vanilla Buttercream Frosting (see page 26), either in a single color or tinted in a variety of shades
1–2 packs of sugar lettering
Candles
Other decorations, such as sugar or chocolate sprinkles, or jimmies

New Baby Cupcakes

A perfect alternative to a bouquet of flowers for new parents, a box of cupcakes would be greatly appreciated and enjoyed. They are straightforward to put together and can be boxed, ribboned, and hand-delivered on your first visit to see the new arrival. You could use one batch of vanilla cupcakes or one batch of lemon cupcakes or half a batch of each.

Make up as many cupcakes as you need to fill your chosen box size. If you are using sugar letters, you can spell out the baby's name on one cupcake or put "baby boy" or "baby girl" over a couple of cupcakes and arrange these in the center of the box.

Then you can decorate the rest of your cupcakes with pinks or blues, or maybe some yellows. Look out for sweet sugar and plastic decorations – ducks, booties, bottles, etc. – in specialty party shops, or even some sugar baby animals, which can often be found in packs on supermarket shelves. Obviously remind people not to eat the plastic decorations!

Allow the cupcakes to set for 30 minutes or so before boxing so the edges are not too sticky. Carefully arrange your cakes in the box, tape down, and tie with ribbon to finish.

1 batch of Vanilla or Lemon Cupcakes (see page 15 or 19), regular size

1 batch of Vanilla Buttercream Frosting (see page 26) – we recommend you keep some uncolored and tint some pale blue or pale pink, depending on the sex of the baby – or Lemon Buttercream Frosting (see page 31)

1 pack of sugar lettering (optional) or other appropriate decorations

White cake box

Ribbons

Christening Cupcakes

Christening cupcakes have become extremely popular. Arranged on a tier, they make a stunning centerpiece for a christening buffet. You can choose any flavor of cake and flavor and color of buttercream frosting. Using our decorating tips and suggestions you can achieve completely professional cupcakes for an intimate gathering or a really large event. Of course, these cupcakes are also ideal served at a wide variety of celebrations, religious or otherwise – bar or bat mitzvahs, naming ceremonies, and so on – as they are always well received.

Batches of cupcakes to cater for the number of guests (plus a few to spare), either regular or mini size

Enough buttercream frosting for the number of cupcakes you decide on

Packs of sugar lettering in blue or pink

Decorations, such as pale sugar sprinkles, sugared rosebuds, or dragees

For a christening we are most often requested to use vanilla or lemon cupcakes (see page 15 or 19) with vanilla or lemon buttercream frosting (see page 26 or 31) kept to natural colors or tinted pale shades of baby blue, soft pink, or lilac.

Simple decoration is key here – sugared letters in blue or pink used to spell out the baby's name on as many cupcakes as desired or the birth or christening date on others is one idea. Pale sugar sprinkles in white, pearl, or pastel shades look sweet, while sugared rosebuds or dainty fresh flowers give a classic, simple, and pretty finish.

As an easy alternative you can purchase dragees in many lovely shades from specialty grocery stores or fine confectionary shops. Your little cakes will look smart and delicious topped with these. Once they are frosted, arrange your cupcakes on a tier or serving plates.

Anniversary Cupcakes

The versatility of cupcakes means they are ideal for absolutely every anniversary, without exception. As before, it's just a question of deciding on flavors (the favorites of the couple, of course) and cleverly decorating to coincide with the appropriate anniversary. Mini cupcakes work well in party situations as they are the perfect finger food and, what's more, you can serve them with either coffee, tea, or champagne.

Before you start to frost the cupcakes, decide on your decorations and message. You could spell out the couple's names and/or the date of the anniversary, in sugared letters, placing one letter or number on each cake, or use numbered candles or sparklers purchased from most party shops; you could even arrange the cakes in the shape of the number of years being celebrated.

Once the cupcakes are frosted and decorated, serve on pretty silver trays, a large silver cake stand, or colored napkins to satisfy the eye and the palate.

As many batches of mini cupcakes as you need for your guests

As many batches of buttercream frosting as you need to top the total number of cupcakes

Decorations to represent the particular anniversary:
- **simple silver or gold sugar balls for 25 and 50 years**
- **edible sugar pearls for 30 years**
- **sugar and crystallized flowers in appropriate colors**
- **fresh flowers, such as daffodils (10 years), roses (15 years), lilies (20 years), sweet peas (30 years), and violets (50 years)**
- **children's plastic rings in the desired color for a diamond, emerald, or ruby anniversary**

Packs of sugar lettering

Candles

Weddings

There can be no surprise that a tier of cupcakes has become super-fashionable and increasingly popular for the most prestigious of all cakes, the wedding cake. With so many decisions to make and other people's opinions to deal with during your wedding planning, using cupcakes for the wedding cake makes life really uncomplicated. Quantities can be left until the last minute when the RSVPs are returned and the bride, groom, and mothers-in-law can all have their favorite flavor on the day.

A tier of wedding cupcakes can take the form of a traditional classic cake or be totally unconventional: the possibilities are endless. After a few straightforward decisions – flavors of cakes and frostings, whether to have a small top cake for cutting, what type of decorations to use – and confirmation of numbers, it's just a matter of simple baking, care and attention with frosting, and a steady hand in construction.

A tier is still the preferred choice to display the cakes, even for the less traditional of weddings, because height is the best way to create impact. For our very classic orders, more often than not we bake vanilla or almond cupcakes with a complementing vanilla or amaretto buttercream. As decoration, edible fresh flowers always look beautiful. You could ask the florist creating the bride's bouquet to make a small posy that can rest upon the top cake, but it's just as effective to place the head of a large hydrangea or fragrant garden roses directly on to the top cake, with buds and petals tucked throughout and a few scattered on the table. Keeping the color scheme consistent and the decoration simple, achieves the effect of one large wedding cake without the tricky cutting, making the whole thing extraordinarily easy for guests to enjoy at the reception or, later, to be individually boxed and presented to guests as they depart.

White Amaretto Cupcakes

These cupcakes are born from the delicious source of sweet almonds that produce the aromatic liqueur Amaretto. Feel free to multiply the quantities for however many cupcakes you need for the wedding.

Makes 12 regular cupcakes

8 tablespoons unsalted butter,
    at room temperature
¾ cup plus 2 tablespoons
    granulated sugar
2 large eggs, free-range or organic
¾ cup plus 2 tablespoons
    self-rising flour
¾ cup plus 1 tablespoon
    all-purpose flour
½ cup 2% reduced-fat milk,
    at room temperature
½ teaspoon Amaretto liqueur or
    almond extract

For the syrup
⅔ cup granulated sugar
½ cup water
½ teaspoon Amaretto liqueur or
    almond extract

To decorate
1 batch of Amaretto Buttercream
    Frosting (see page 119)
Toasted slivered almonds, other
    decorations, or unsprayed
    edible flowers

Preheat the oven to 350°F and line a 12-cup muffin pan with cupcake liners.

In a large mixing bowl cream the butter and sugar until the mixture is pale and smooth, which should take 3–5 minutes using an electric hand mixer. Add the eggs, one at a time, mixing for a few minutes after each addition.

Sift the two flours together into a separate bowl. Mix the milk and the Amaretto together. Add one-third of the flours to the creamed mixture and beat well. Pour in one-third of the milk and beat again. Repeat these steps until all the flour and milk have been added.

Carefully spoon the mixture into the cups, filling them about two-thirds full. Bake in the oven for about 25 minutes until slightly raised and golden brown. To check they are cooked, insert a wooden skewer in the center of one of the cupcakes – it should come out clean.

Meanwhile, combine the ingredients for the syrup in a microwave-safe bowl and microwave on high until the sugar melts completely (about 1½ minutes); stir to combine. Alternatively heat over a low heat in a saucepan.

Remove the cupcakes from the oven and leave in the pan for about 10 minutes before carefully placing on a wire rack. While they are still warm, dip the tops of the cupcakes into the syrup for a couple of seconds. Return to the wire rack to cool completely.

Top these cupcakes with amaretto buttercream frosting and finish with toasted slivered almonds or, for a wedding, use the decorations or fresh flowers chosen by the bride and groom.

Amaretto Buttercream Frosting

Perhaps it is the inspired romance brought to the senses by the warm, subtle taste and smell of this frosting that makes the Amaretto cupcakes a hugely popular choice by impending brides and grooms for the most romantic cake of all! Multiply the recipe according to the number of cupcakes you need to frost.

In a large mixing bowl beat the butter, milk, vanilla extract, and half the confectioners' sugar until smooth – this will take a few minutes using an electric hand mixer. Gradually add the remainder of the confectioners' sugar to produce a buttercream of a creamy and smooth consistency.

Add the Amaretto and beat well. You should taste the frosting at this stage as you may wish to add another ¼ teaspoon to make it a little stronger.

The buttercream can be stored in an airtight container for up to 3 days at room temperature. Before re-using, beat well.

Makes enough to frost
15–20 regular cupcakes or
about 60 mini cupcakes

8 tablespoons unsalted butter,
   at room temperature
¼ cup 2% reduced-fat milk,
   at room temperature
1 teapoon pure vanilla extract
5 cups confectioners' sugar, sifted
¼ teaspoon Amaretto liqueur
   or almond extract (this could
   be increased according to your
   preference)

"Non-traditional" Wedding Cupcakes

For a less traditional affair, many flavors and colors can be mixed. Everything is much less formal: family and friends can help themselves to the flavor they fancy – a choice other cakes cannot offer. And the decorations can definitely be different: how about mini cupcakes topped with old-fashioned candy hearts or regular cupcakes adorned with confetti-shaped sprinkles? Simple but effective. There really is no limit to what can be used to represent the bride and groom and the atmosphere they want to create. As an example, we recently delivered a tower of chocolate malted cupcakes in varying sizes, all topped with plastic elephants, and attached to each one was a tiny luggage label with the couple's names handwritten on!

For these less traditional wedding cupcakes on the right, we have used a beautiful silver tier and brightly colored roses. We once provided wedding cupcakes for a lovely summer wedding in a tent in the middle of a field, where we set out the cakes on a variety of vintage glass cake stands surrounded by jugs of wild summer flowers.

Before starting, decide on the quantities, flavors, and decorations you are going to use. A mix of regular and mini cupcakes is always fun. You could use a complete mixture of flavors of cake, types of frosting, and decorations – sprinkles, sugar flowers, sugar hearts, candies, lettering, figurines, and so on.

Bake, frost, and decorate the cupcakes and then decide where the tier or stands will be shown at the reception. Place all the cupcakes on the tier as you wish, mixing up the colors and flavors randomly to create a colorful, pretty, and delicious display.

"Traditional" Wedding Cupcakes

For this tier of wedding cupcakes we have used a simple plexiglass tier, made of flat plexiglass plates in varying sizes and interlocking plexiglass pieces that create the central spine of the tier. With tiers such as this you can use as many of the levels as you need, depending on the size of the wedding and the number of cupcakes needed. It is also very unobtrusive and so does not detract from the visual sophistication of the cupcakes.

Make the number of cupcakes required, either in regular or mini size or a mixture of the two. We would recommend either the Amaretto cupcakes (see page 116) or simple vanilla cupcakes (see page 15) with vanilla buttercream (see page 26), left in its natural cream color. Decide whether you want a top cake for the bride and groom to cut and, if so, what size – the one shown in the picture here is 6 inches in size, but an 8-inch size would work just as well. The top cake could be made in either chocolate or vanilla cake and then covered with the same vanilla buttercream you use on the cupcakes.

Make, frost, and decorate the top cake first and leave it to sit for a while to allow it to set a little. It is best placed on a silver cake board before frosting, which will make it much easier to lift in when placing on the tier and then off again, depending on how much is eaten! Then frost the cupcakes and decorate with the sugar flowers you have chosen. Get the florist to make up a small bouquet for the top cake and to leave you some spare edible flowers on the wedding day once they have finished creating the arrangements for the wedding.

Assemble the tier in the exact position where the cakes will be displayed for the wedding reception as it is not advisable to attempt to move it once it has been set up. Carefully place the cupcakes throughout the layers, mixing up the different sizes and not spacing them out too much, as they look much better when they are quite tightly packed. Place the top cake carefully on to the top level. To finish, arrange your bouquet of flowers in the center of the top cake. Step back from the display to check it looks okay and then dot some extra flowers or foliage throughout the tier or on the table.

Beyond Cupcakes

Much as we love making cupcakes, there are days when it is still nice to bake a layer cake. In our shops we always have a wide selection of layer cakes available by the slice or whole. Quite often our customers order a layer cake and some cupcakes, and at other times a simple jelly roll or rich chocolate cake fits the bill.

You can bake our selection of layer cakes for a special occasion or for a treat with coffee. You can also make the cakes in larger sizes than the 8-inch size we recommend if you have a large number to feed – double the recipe to make two 10- or 12-inch layer cakes that can serve 20–25 people easily.

SWEET! SWEET!

Chocolate Layer Cake

Although slightly more involved than some of our cupcake recipes, this deliciously moist chocolate cake is well worth the effort. It makes a fantastic birthday or celebration dessert, and is always the first choice of all our children.

Makes two 8-inch cakes

8oz bittersweet chocolate (70% cocoa solids)

12 tablespoons unsalted butter, at room temperature

2 cups packed light brown sugar

3 large eggs, free-range or organic, separated

2⅔ cups all-purpose flour, sifted

1½ teaspoons baking powder

1½ teaspoons baking soda

½ teaspoon salt

2 cups 2% reduced-fat milk, at room temperature

2 teaspoons pure vanilla extract

To decorate

1 batch of Chocolate or Vanilla Buttercream Frosting (see page 26 or 29)

Chocolate sprinkles or other sugar decorations

Preheat the oven to 375°F. Grease and line two 8-inch cake pans with parchment paper.

Break the chocolate into pieces and place in a microwave-safe bowl. Melt on medium in 30-second intervals until completely melted. Stir well between each session. Alternatively, place the chocolate in a heatproof bowl over a saucepan of barely simmering water. Stir occasionally until completely melted. Set the bowl aside to cool.

In a large mixing bowl cream the butter and sugar until the mixture is pale and smooth, which should take 3–5 minutes using an electric hand mixer. Put the egg yolks in a separate bowl and beat them for several minutes. Slowly add the egg yolks to the creamed butter and sugar and beat well. Add the cooled chocolate to this mixture and again beat well.

Combine the flour, baking powder, baking soda, and salt in a separate bowl. Mix the milk and vanilla extract together. Add one-third of the flour to the creamed mixture and beat well. Pour in one-third of the milk and beat again. Repeat these steps until all the flour and milk have been added.

In a clean bowl with clean beaters, whip the egg whites until soft peaks start to form. Carefully fold the eggs whites into the main batter using a rubber spatula. (Do not beat or you will take all the air out of the mixture.) Divide the mixture evenly between the pans and bake for about 30 minutes. Insert a wooden skewer in the center of one of the cakes – it should come out clean.

Remove from the oven and leave the cakes in the pans for 10 minutes before turning out on to a wire rack to cool. Peel the parchment paper from the bases of the cakes. Once they are cool, sandwich the layers together with vanilla or chocolate buttercream frosting and cover the top of the cake with more. Decorate with chocolate sprinkles or other sugar decorations.

The baked cake layers can be wrapped in plastic wrap before frosting and will keep at room temperature for up to 3 days or you can freeze them, wrapped, and defrost when needed.

Vanilla Layer Cake

This vanilla layer cake is one of our bakery staples that we are frequently asked for and if you make it in a food processor it takes no time at all. As with most vanilla cake recipes, the list of ingredients is fairly standard, but factor in good-quality ingredients, careful measuring and weighing, and setting the correct oven temperatures, and the result is fantastic. We use this as the basis of many a birthday cake, not least because it can be frosted and decorated to any effect.

Preheat the oven to 350°F. Grease and line two 8-inch cake pans with parchment paper.

Put the butter, sugar, flour, cornstarch, and baking powder into a food processor. Pulse for a few seconds until evenly mixed. Add the remaining ingredients gradually, processing briefly until just combined. Don't be tempted to overmix or you will take all the air out of the batter.

If you prefer, you can prepare the mixture with an electric hand mixer. Cream the butter and sugar in a bowl until the mixture is pale and smooth – this should take 3–5 minutes. Combine the dry ingredients in a separate bowl. Add the eggs to the creamed mixture, one at a time, mixing for a few minutes after each addition, alternating with the dry ingredients, and finally the vanilla extract and the milk. Beat well after each addition, but again do not overbeat.

Divide the mixture evenly between the pans and bake in the oven for about 25 minutes until raised and golden brown. Insert a wooden skewer in the center of one of the cakes – it should come out clean. Remove from the oven and leave the cakes in the pans for about 10 minutes before turning out on to a wire rack to cool. Peel the parchment paper from the bases of the cakes.

Once they are cool, sandwich the layers together with half of the buttercream frosting and cover the top of the cake with the rest. Decorate the cake with whatever fits with your occasion. As an alternative, sandwich the cakes with a thin layer of strawberry or raspberry jam and some vanilla buttercream (uncolored), or with freshly whipped cream and some sliced strawberries and dust the top with confectioners' sugar.

Makes two 8-inch cakes

1 cup (2 sticks) unsalted butter, at room temperature
1 cup plus 2 tablespoons granulated sugar
1½ cups self-rising flour, sifted
3 tablespoons cornstarch
1 teaspoon baking powder
4 large eggs, free-range or organic
1 teaspoon pure vanilla extract
3 tablespoons 2% reduced-fat milk, at room temperature

To decorate – choose one of the following:
• 1 batch of any Buttercream Frosting (see pages 26–37)
• 3 tablespoons strawberry or raspberry jam and 1 batch of Vanilla Buttercream Frosting (see page 26)
• Whipped cream and fresh strawberries, plus confectioners' sugar, for dusting

Coffee and Walnut Cake

For a most delicious coffee cake, we adapted this inspired cake from one of Delia Smith's recipes. Combined with our coffee buttercream, it is a coffee-cake connoisseur's delight.

Preheat the oven to 375°F. Grease and line two 8-inch cake pans with parchment paper.

In a large mixing bowl cream the butter and sugar until the mixture is pale and smooth, which should take 3–5 minutes using an electric hand mixer. Add the eggs, one at a time, mixing for a few minutes after each addition. Add the flour and baking powder and beat well.

Grind the walnuts in a food processor for about 30 seconds or so – they should not be too fine. Add the coffee and ground walnuts to the batter and mix again but for no more than 3–4 seconds. The mixture should have a marbled effect and it is very important not to overmix or you will take all the air out of the batter.

Divide the mixture evenly between the pans and bake in the oven for about 25 minutes until raised and golden brown. Insert a wooden skewer in the center of one of the cakes – it should come out clean.

Remove from the oven and let the cakes cool in the pans. Make up the syrup by combining the ingredients in a jug and stirring well to ensure the sugar dissolves completely. After 10–15 minutes, prick the cakes with a fork, brush on the syrup and leave it to soak in.

When you are ready to frost the cakes, carefully turn them out of the pans and peel the parchment paper from the bases. Place one cake on a plate and spread a thin layer of coffee buttercream over it. Place the second cake on top and use the rest of the buttercream to cover the upper surface. Decorate with the walnut halves around the edge.

Makes two 8-inch cakes

12 tablespoon unsalted butter, at room temperature
¾ cup plus 1 tablespoon sugar, preferably golden bakers'
3 large eggs, free-range or organic
1 cup plus 2 tablespoons self-rising flour, sifted
1½ teaspoons baking powder
3oz walnuts
1½ tablespoons instant coffee mixed with 2 tablespoons boiling water, cooled

For the syrup
1 tablespoon instant coffee
¼ cup demerara sugar
¼ cup boiling water

To decorate
1½ batches of Coffee Buttercream Frosting (see page 32)
10–12 walnut halves

Lemon Layer Cake

Choose big, juicy lemons and we promise you a deliciously zesty and lively lemon sponge.

Makes two 8-inch cakes

1 cup plus 2 tablespoons
   sugar, preferably golden
   bakers'
1½ cups self-rising flour,
   sifted
1½ teaspoons baking powder
3 tablespoons cornstarch
1 cup (2 sticks) unsalted
   butter, at room
   temperature
4 large eggs, free-range or
   organic
Grated zest and juice of
   2 large juicy lemons
   (otherwise use 3 lemons)

To decorate
1 batch of Lemon
   Buttercream Frosting
   (see page 31)
Sugared lemon slices and/or
   yellow sugar flowers
Grated lemon zest (optional)

Preheat the oven to 375°F. Grease and line two 8-inch cake pans with parchment paper.

Put the sugar, flour, baking powder, and cornstarch in a food processor. Pulse for about 4 seconds until evenly mixed. Add the remaining ingredients and process briefly until evenly blended (roughly 10 seconds). Don't be tempted to overmix.

If you prefer, you can prepare the mixture with an electric hand mixer. Cream the butter and sugar in a bowl until the mixture is pale and smooth. Combine the dry ingredients in a separate bowl. Add the eggs to the creamed mixture, one at a time, mixing for a few minutes after each addition, alternating with the dry ingredients, and finally the grated zest and lemon juice. Beat well after each addition, but again do not overbeat.

Divide the mixture evenly between the pans and bake in the oven for about 25 minutes until raised and golden brown. Insert a wooden skewer in the center of one of the cakes – it should come out clean. Remove from the oven and leave the cakes in the pans for about 10 minutes before turning out on to a wire rack to cool. Peel the parchment paper from the bases of the cakes.

Once they are cool, sandwich the layers together with lemon buttercream frosting and cover the top of the cake with more. Decorate with sugared lemon slices or some yellow sugar flowers or both. You could also use some freshly grated lemon zest if you plan to serve the cake immediately, but be aware it will wilt if left too long!

Decorations

Decorating your cupcakes is the time to be at your most imaginative and creative. After the patience and preciseness required to create a perfect cake and batch of frosting, much fun can be had in choosing decorations to complete the picture. You should spend some time thinking about what would be appropriate for the particular cupcakes you are going to make and the occasion they will be eaten at and then tailor your choice of decoration accordingly. You do not need to spend a lot of money on decorations if you are clever with your choices, or need any special skills to decorate, and can make the finished product as simple or as complicated and extravagant as you want.

Almost anything can be used as a cake decoration. It certainly does not always need to be edible, as plastic figurines or fresh flowers can be equally pretty (just don't let anyone try to eat them!). In the last five years it has become much easier to buy a huge selection of sugar cake decorations. Most craft and party shops now stock sugar sprinkles in a variety of colors, packets of sugar animals and sugar flowers, crystallized rose and violet petals, gold and silver dragees, chocolate curls, coffee beans, chocolate and liqueur truffles, candles, plastic cake toppers and figurines, and other decorations that can be sought out through the aisles.

As shown in our recipe for sweetie cupcakes (see page 102) you can use any variety of candy or chocolate to decorate your cupcakes, all of which can be bought from the local confectioner or chocolate shop. For the cupcakes made using fresh fruits, you can use the grated zest of oranges, lemons, or limes to decorate, or whole strawberries or raspberries.

One of the advantages of using buttercream frosting on cupcakes is that it is much easier to decorate, as it never sets completely hard and gives a much better and deeper surface with which to experiment. If you are unhappy with what you have done, you can simply remove the decorations and start again. Equally, if you feel you are not particularly good at frosting, you can easily use decorations to cover up any mistakes – simply use a few more sprinkles and no one will ever know.

If you are making cupcakes with children, it is a good idea to let them be in charge of the decorating at the end. Allow them to throw on whatever they have chosen – although it's probably safer to use smaller sugar sprinkles if the children are small – and it will fill an enjoyable afternoon and create a colorful and delicious treat.

At the other end of the scale, if decorating your own or somebody else's wedding cupcakes, take extra care when choosing the decorations and make sure you have bought them some time in advance (unless using fresh flowers of course) so there is no disappointment on the day.

However, whatever kind of decorations you decide on, just remember to have fun with them and look around for the most interesting and original ones you can find. It is a very personal choice and different people like completely different things, so you should always go with your instincts and be sure it will work out brilliantly. We have found choosing the decorations for our cupcakes one of the most enjoyable things we do and still feel delight when we chance upon something new.

Techniques

We want to share the techniques we have found to be most useful in achieving success with our Primrose Bakery cupcakes and layer cakes.

• Sourcing the best quality ingredients at your disposal and budget will make a big difference to the end result. These include free-range or organic eggs, whole or 2% reduced-fat milk, and a good-quality unsalted butter. If organic is your first choice, you will find that organic confectioners' sugar will not produce the creamy buttercreams we make. It is unfortunately grainy and, in its natural state, discolored, making it impossible to produce the pretty pastels we prefer to use.

• Correct storage is paramount with pantry ingredients to ensure longevity and freshness. Remember to check use-by dates, especially on ingredients not regularly used and on spices and extracts that remain on the shelf because of the small quantities needed at any one time. Airtight containers with lock-on lids are the best way of keeping dry ingredients as well as storing finished cupcakes overnight. If you choose to freeze unfrosted cupcakes, do this when they are completely cool. Never be tempted to store frosted cupcakes in the refrigerator as this will spoil their freshness of flavor and texture. If baking in the summer, frost at the last possible moment and keep in the coolest shade available.

• Before starting to bake, it is best to bring all ingredients to room temperature. Butter should be soft and malleable: by leaving out the correct quantity for 30 minutes or so before baking you should have the perfect consistency. Make sure the oven is at the correct temperature before putting the cupcakes in and always try not to open the oven door while they are baking.

• Careful measuring of ingredients can make a huge difference too, so don't be tempted to guess at quantities too much or add in something extra on a whim!

• It is most important to have plenty of time and patience when baking and really enjoy what you are doing – that way your cupcakes will turn out brilliantly and can be enjoyed by all, including yourself.

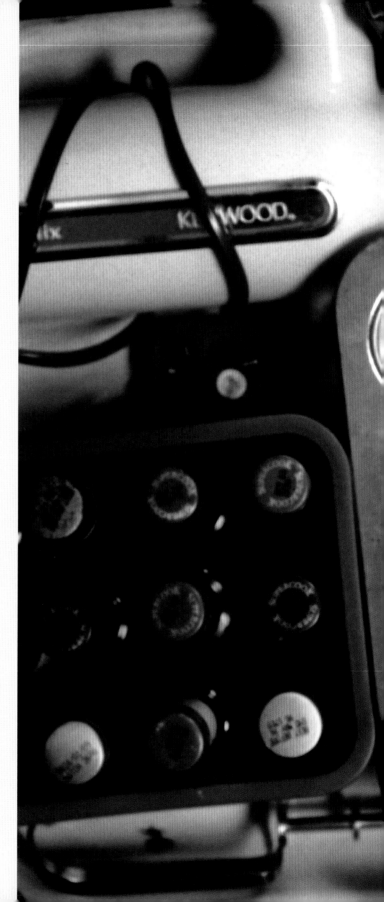

Utensils/Equipment

You certainly do not need every piece of equipment on this list to bake perfect cupcakes – it is more a suggestion of some of the things we think you will find useful for baking of all kinds. We do feel an electric mixer is very useful, making the process easier and quicker.

Large mixing bowls

Measuring spoons

Measuring cups (dry and liquid)

Electric hand mixer

Food processor

Sieve

Grater

Muffin pans (regular and mini size)

Paper cupcake liners (regular and mini size)

Spatulas, rubber or silicone

Wooden spoons

Cake testers – a wooden skewer will do

Wire cooling racks

Parchment paper

Plastic wrap

8-inch cake pans with removable bottoms or
    springform pans

Small or large metal frosting spatulas, both offset and plain

Airtight containers

Oven timer

Baking sheets

Index

Primrose Bakery

www.primrosebakery.org.uk

Cafe, cupcakes to order, candles, toys, cards, tableware

Primrose Hill: 69 Gloucester Avenue, London NW1 8LD

Tel: 020 7483 4222

Covent Garden: 42 Tavistock Street, London WC2E 7PB

Tel: 020 7836 3638

Email: primrose-bakery@btconnect.com

Sources

Amazon

www.amazon.com

An excellent source for many ingredients and decorations, including candied violets and rose petals

The Baker's Nook

www.shopbakersnook.com

902 W. Michigan

Saline, MI

(734) 429-1320

Edible decorations, cupcake liners, pans, food coloring

Chefshop.com

www.chefshop.com

P.O. Box 3488

Seattle, WA 98114

(800) 596-0885

Golden bakers' sugar in large quantities, as well as top quality rose water, orange blossom water, and vanilla extract

Country Kitchen Sweetart

www.countrykitchensa.com

4621 Speedway Drive

Fort Wayne, IN 46825

(800) 497-3927

Edible decorations, cupcake liners, pans, food coloring

eAlpha Enterprise

www.ecrafta.com

438 W. Grant St.

Calexico, CA 92231

(888) 327-2382

Plastic figurines for topping shower, wedding, sweet sixteen, and other special occasion cupcakes

Millcreek Country Stores

www.millcreekcountrystore.com

Newmanstown, PA 17073

(610) 589-9492

All kinds of edible garnishes, such as sprinkles, nonpareils, dragees, and colored sugar

The Party Works

www.thepartyworks.com

1967 Hwy 395 S

Chewelah, WA 99109

(877) 887-2789

Assorted 3D sugar shapes, from animals to flowers

Pattycakes

www.shop.pattycakes.com

34-55 Junction Blvd

Jackson Heights, NY 11372-3828

(866) 999-8400

Cupcake accessories, including many plastic toppers and figurines, cardboard boxes, and more

Sugarcraft

www.sugarcraft.com

3665 Dixie Hwy

Hamilton, OH 45015

Just about everything you will need for making cupcakes, including a good selection of stands

Wilton Industries

www.wilton.com

2240 West 75th Street

Woodridge, IL 60517

(800) 794-5866

One-stop shopping for cupcake liners, sugar decorations, and more